LIVING IN THE WILD: BIG CATS

LIONS

Claire Throp

Heinemann
LIBRARY
Chicago, Illinois

Edited by Clare Lewis and Adrian Vigliano
Designed by Tim Bond
Original illustrations © HL Studios
Picture research by Tracy Cummins
Originated by Capstone Global Library Ltd
Printed in CTPS

17 16 15 14 13
10 9 8 7 6 5 4 3 2 1

Library of Congress Cataloging-in-Publication Data

Throp, Claire, author.
  Lions / Claire Throp.
       pages cm.—(Living in the wild. Big cats)
  Summary: "Here's an animal lover's one-stop source for in-depth
information on lions! What do they eat? How do they behave? Are
they at risk? This book also includes loads of fun and fascinating facts
about lions, as well as maps, charts, and wonderful photographs of
these clever creatures."—Provided by publisher.
  Includes bibliographical references and index.
  ISBN 978-1-4329-8108-2 (hb)—ISBN 978-1-4329-8120-4 (pb) 1.
Lion—Juvenile literature. I. Title.

  QL737.C23T47383 2014
  599.757—dc23   2013013123

Acknowledgments

The author and publisher are grateful to the following for permission to
reproduce copyright material:
Alamy p. 33 (© Martin Harvey); Dreamstime.com p. 10d (© Chris
Moncrieff); Flickr p. 10b (Karen Stout); Getty Images pp. 7 (Stuart
Westmorland), 11 (Luciano Candisani), 13 (Purestock), 15 (Art Wolfe),
16 (Richard Packwood), 23 (Ariadne Van Zandbergen), 25 (Susann
Parker), 27 (Andy Rouse), 35 (Doug Steakley), 36 (AFP/Getty Images),
40 (Ian Cumming); Shutterstock pp. 5, 10f (EcoPrint), 6 (Sue Green),
10a (Eduard Kyslynskyy), 10c (Howard Klaaste), 10e (Volodymyr
Burdiak), 10g (Lilyana Vynogradova), 10h (Graur Razvan), 17
(Stanislav Duben), 18, 30 (Ludmila Yilmaz), 19 (e2dan), 22 (clickit),
24 (Stu Porter), 31 (Dave Pusey), 32 (Oleg Znamenskiy), 39 (Tiberius
Dinu); Superstock pp. 29 (Juniors), 38 (Ton Koene / age footstock), 41
(NHPA), 43 (Minden Pictures), 45 (Gerard Lacz / age footstock).

Cover photograph of a lion reproduced with permission of Superstock
(age fotostock).

We would like to thank Michael Bright for his invaluable help in the
preparation of this book.

Every effort has been made to contact copyright holders of any
material reproduced in this book. Any omissions will be rectified in
subsequent printings if notice is given to the publisher.

Disclaimer

Contents

Some words are shown in bold, **like this**. You can find out what they mean by looking in the glossary.

What Are Big Cats?

Have you ever heard a lion's roar? It can be pretty scary! A male lion will roar to warn another male to stay off his **territory**. A lion's roar can be heard from 5 miles (8 kilometers) away.

Mammals

Big cats such as lions are mammals. Mammals have fur or hair on their body and use lungs to breathe. They give birth to live young and babies feed on milk from their mother. Does this description sound familiar? It should—humans are also mammals.

Cats

There are 36 **species** in the cat family, including the **domestic** cat you might have at home! But only a small number are known informally as big cats. One definition of big cats includes all the species of *Panthera* or roaring cats. Tigers are the largest of the roaring cats, followed by lions, jaguars, and leopards. Some scientists also describe the cheetah, puma, snow leopard, and clouded leopard as big cats.

WALKING ON AIR

If you watch a lion walking, its heels don't touch the ground! The toes are big compared to the rest of the paw. Pads on the bottom of their feet cushion their feet and allow them to move more quietly.

Cats are great hunters, usually searching for food at night because their vision is often a lot better than that of their **prey** and because it's cooler. All their senses are excellent, helped by rotating ears and sensitive vibrissae (whiskers).

Lion cubs might look cute, but when they grow older they will have to become killers in order to survive.

What Are Lions?

A lion's fur is usually light brown, although lions with white fur can be found in some areas, particularly the Timbavati region of South Africa. Lions have large teeth and **retractable** claws, which are both useful for hunting. They also have very powerful front legs. Females are known as lionesses.

Most male lions have manes—no other big cat has a mane. Manes can vary in color and size. Some lions in the Tsavo area of Kenya don't have manes at all, but others may have manes that reach to their stomachs.

Lions are the most **social** cats.

Characteristics

Lions live in groups called prides. They are **nocturnal**, meaning they are more active at night than during the day. Lions are carnivores, which means they eat meat. They can run fast—up to 36 miles (58 kilometers) per hour—but only for short distances.

Lion size

Males lions are bigger than females—in length and height. The height of a lion is measured to its shoulder.

	Female lion	Male lion
Length	4.9ft (1.5m)	5.9–6.9ft (1.8–2.1m)
Height	3–3.6ft (0.9–1.1m)	3.9ft (1.2m)
Weight	220–360 lbs (100–164 kg)	326–470 lbs (148–213 kg)

HOW LONG

A lion's tail can be 3 feet (1 meter) long! The tail has a tuft of longer hair on the tip that is usually darker than the rest of a lion's fur.

Manes usually get darker and longer as a lion grows older.

How Are Lions Classified?

Classification is the way that humans try to make sense of the natural world. Grouping living things together by the characteristics that they share allows us to identify them and understand why they live where they do and behave how they do.

Classification groups

In classification, animals are split into various groups. The standard groups are Kingdom, Phylum, Class, Order, Family, Genus, and Species. Sometimes, further classification involves adding more groups such as a sub-order or infra-order. Each of the standard groups contains fewer and fewer members. For example, there are far more animals to be found in the class Mammalia (mammals) as animals in the family Felidae (cats). Animals are given an internationally recognized two-part Latin name. This helps to avoid confusion if animals are known by different common names in different countries. The lion's Latin name is *Panthera leo*, for example.

CLOSE RELATIVES

Tigers are lions' closest relatives. Their bodies are very similar and only experts could tell them apart if it wasn't for the different colors and markings of their fur.

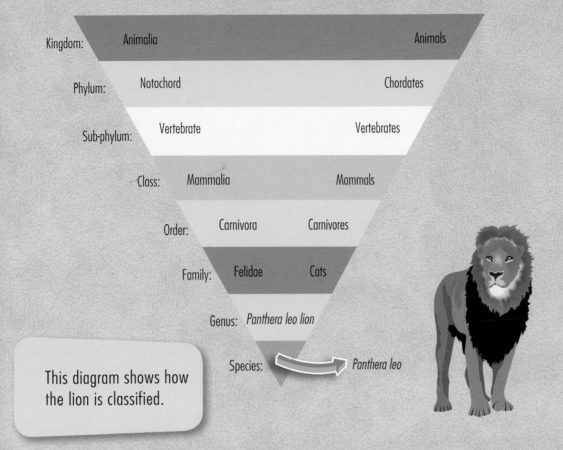

Kingdom:	Animalia	Animals
Phylum:	Notochord	Chordates
Sub-phylum:	Vertebrate	Vertebrates
Class:	Mammalia	Mammals
Order:	Carnivora	Carnivores
Family:	Felidae	Cats
Genus:	*Panthera leo lion*	
Species:		*Panthera leo*

This diagram shows how the lion is classified.

Classification disagreements

Lions are divided into African (*Panthera leo leo*) and Asiatic (*Panthera leo persica*) subspecies. These two subspecies separated about 100,000 years ago. Some scientists think that African lions can be split into five subspecies based on where they live. However, this is not universally agreed. There are some visual differences between lions in the different regions. Lions in West and Central Africa are smaller, have smaller manes, and may have different shaped skulls than lions that live in East and southern Africa. Asiatic lions are generally smaller than the African subspecies and have smaller, darker manes.

Evolution of cats

While the first cat-like mammals appeared 60 million years ago, it is thought that the first true cats appeared about 25 million years ago. One was Proailurus, meaning "early cat," which was an animal the size of a large domestic cat. The family Felidae includes modern wild cats such as lions and other big cats as well as domestic cats. Members of this family are called felids.

This feline family tree shows estimated dates of when new lines **evolved**.

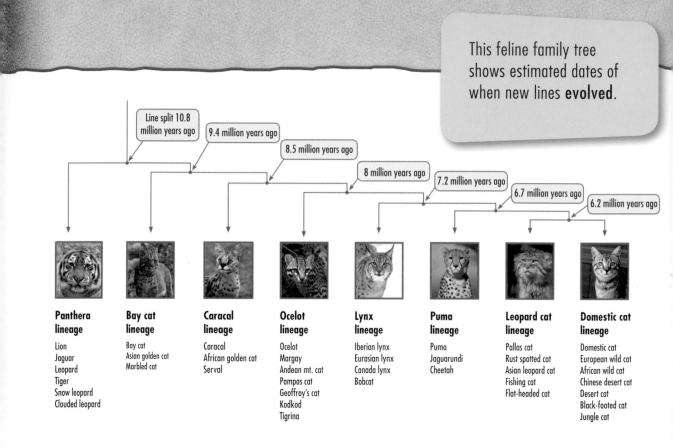

Panthera lineage

Lion
Jaguar
Leopard
Tiger
Snow leopard
Clouded leopard

Bay cat lineage

Bay cat
Asian golden cat
Marbled cat

Caracal lineage

Caracal
African golden cat
Serval

Ocelot lineage

Ocelot
Margay
Andean mt. cat
Pampas cat
Geoffroy's cat
Kodkod
Tigrina

Lynx lineage

Iberian lynx
Eurasian lynx
Canada lynx
Bobcat

Puma lineage

Puma
Jaguarundi
Cheetah

Leopard cat lineage

Pallas cat
Rust spotted cat
Asian leopard cat
Fishing cat
Flat-headed cat

Domestic cat lineage

Domestic cat
European wild cat
African wild cat
Chinese desert cat
Desert cat
Black-footed cat
Jungle cat

Labels on family tree:
Line split 10.8 million years ago
9.4 million years ago
8.5 million years ago
8 million years ago
7.2 million years ago
6.7 million years ago
6.2 million years ago

Extinct in the wild

In the past, other subspecies of lion existed such as the Barbary and Cape lions, but they are now **extinct** in the wild. However, there are thought to be some Barbary lions held in **captivity** and the possibility of other extinct subspecies held somewhere in captivity.

White lions are not **albinos**; they just have white fur.

LINDA TUCKER

Linda Tucker is a **conservationist**, author, and the founder of the Global White Lion Protection Trust, which she set up in 2002. After an encounter with some lions while on holiday in Timbavati, Linda gave up her career in advertising in London and returned to South Africa. She saved a white lion cub from a canned hunting camp (where animals are kept in enclosed areas specifically to be hunted) after a long battle in court. Then, with the help of a donation from Sheryl Leach, creator of the children's TV character, Barney, the purple dinosaur, protected land was bought for the now fully-grown lion and its cubs. Today, Tucker is still fighting to protect the white lion.

Where Do Lions Live?

A habitat is the place where an animal lives. The habitat has to provide everything the animal needs from food to shelter. An animal is dependent on its habitat.

Lions mainly live in sub-Saharan Africa. There is also one small forest in northwest India—the Gir Forest—where about 300 lions can be found.

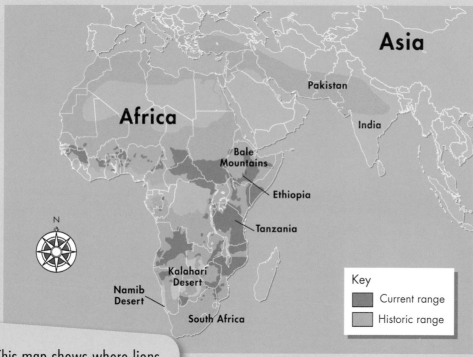

This map shows where lions live now: Africa and the Gir Forest in India. It also shows the historic range of lions. It is clear how much land they have lost.

POPULATION DECREASE

A hundred years ago there were thought to be 200,000 lions in Africa. Now there are less than 30,000.

Lions often live in areas where there are trees and shrubs to provide shelter for their cubs.

Habitat

Lions can live in many different habitats: prairie, forest, semi-desert, and mountainous habitats. Very few lions live in rainforest, but there is a small group living in the montane rainforests and cloud forests of the Kafa Biosphere **Reserve** in Ethiopia. Lions are not common in desert regions either but they can be found in the Namib Desert in southern Africa. Usually, lions like to live near water because that attracts a wider selection of prey for them to eat. Lions themselves must also have access to water for they generally drink daily and usually drink after eating, although they can go for several days without water.

Some lions live at high altitudes, which means they live high above sea level. A very small number of lions—the Harenna Forest group of lions—have been found living in the Bale Mountains in Ethiopia at a height of about 13,910 feet (4,240 meters). In India, Asiatic lions live in teak forest and grassland.

What Adaptations Help Lions Survive?

An adaptation is something that allows an animal to live in a particular place in a particular way. Adaptations arise over thousands of years as animal species evolve.

A lion's body

A lion's body is **adapted** particularly to help it hunt. Huge shoulder muscles and powerful front legs help in catching and bringing down large prey. Lions also have big paws with curved retractable claws that help them to grab and hold on to prey. Retractable claws are usually hidden inside the lion's paw. This helps to keep them sharp and prevents them wearing away as the lion moves around. When needed, the lion can choose to pull the claws out. A lion's front claws can be nearly 1.5 inches (4 centimeters) long.

Most lions have light brown or golden fur that allows them to hide easily in long grasses. This camouflage helps the lions **stalk** prey without the prey animal knowing they are there.

HOW LIONS COOL DOWN

Humans sweat to help them cool down on a hot day, but lions do not have enough sweat glands to keep them cool. Instead they pant—up to 200 times a minute! They may also lie on their backs as their belly has thinner skin over it, which allows more heat to leave their body.

This well camouflaged lion is stalking its prey.

Stomach

A lion has a distensible stomach. This means its stomach can easily expand, or get bigger, which allows it to eat large meals (similar to a human eating 272 chicken breasts!) in one go. This is useful because the lion does not know how long it will be before it eats again.

One of the differences between African and Asiatic lions is that Asiatic lions all have a fold of skin on their belly. This means they don't get injured as easily if they are kicked by prey because there is more cushioning. Only some African lions have this fold of skin.

Jaws and teeth

Lions have very powerful jaws and four long, pointed canine teeth that can puncture the flesh of prey without the lion having to use too much force. A lion's tongue has backward facing spines, called papillae, that are used to scrape food off the bones of their prey. They are also used for **grooming** fur. You might have seen them on a pet cat's tongue.

Adult lions have 30 teeth.

WHISKER SPOTS

Lions can be identified by whisker spots that are unique to each lion. Whisker spots can be found on either side of the face in several rows. Two rows are used in identification. The top full row of spots is called the reference row. A row with a smaller number of spots above the reference row is the identification row. There can be up to five spots in this row and it is their position in relation to the reference row that is particularly important in identifying lions. Researchers can use photographs of the lions to identify them.

LION GUARDIANS

Dr Leelah Hazzah set up the Lion Guardians project in East Africa in 2007. Maasai warriors have traditionally seen lion hunting as an important ritual. Lions are also speared in revenge if they have killed **livestock**. Warriors who have become Lion Guardians now help to save lions rather than kill them. The warriors monitor lion numbers, help herders to avoid areas where lions have recently been seen, improve protection for livestock, and educate other Maasai about the tourism value of lions and other carnivores. The warriors have been very successful in preventing lion deaths in the areas in which they work, stopping 45 hunting parties in 2010 alone.

Senses

Lions have very good vision. Forward-facing eyes show they are **predators**. This positioning of the eyes allows lions to judge distances better, which is useful for hunting.

Their hearing is also excellent, helped by ears that can rotate from side to side, allowing lions to hear distant sounds from all directions. They can hear prey that is more than 1 mile (1.5 kilometers) away.

Lions have a vomeronasal organ on the roof of their mouth that is used for identifying different chemical messages. They make a face, known as Flehmen's response, when using this organ. They open their mouth, lift their chin and wrinkle their nose to allow air—and the scent—to flow over the organ. You may have seen pet cats make an odd open-mouthed face. It is helpful for detecting territorial scent marks, finding prey, and working out when a female is ready to mate.

AGE ESTIMATION

The age of a lion can be estimated by several means, one of which is the color of the nose. Young lions have very pink noses, but more and more black speckles appear as the lion gets older. Tooth wear and how long a male lion's mane is also helps in guessing age.

A lion's eyes are six times more sensitive to light than a human's eyes. This means lions can see much better than humans can in dim light.

REFLECTIVE EYES

A light-reflecting layer of cells in a lion's eyes, called tapetum lucidum, helps them to see at night. The layer acts like a mirror, reflecting what the lion sees back into its eyes, so it gets a second chance to see it.

What Do Lions Eat?

Living things in any habitat depend on each other. This is called interdependence. Animals eat other animals or plants in order to get energy. They in turn may be eaten by bigger animals. These links between animals and plants are called food chains. Many connected food chains add up to a food web.

A food chain starts with a plant because plants are the only organisms that can make their own food. They are called producers. Consumers eat plants or other animals. Lions are consumers and they are called carnivores because they eat meat. Animals that eat other animals are known as predators. The animals they eat are known as prey.

Predators

Fully-grown lions have no natural predators—except humans. Hyenas and other larger mammals sometimes kill weak or young lions.

Lions can eat mammals of all sizes but prefer medium to large animals, such as wildebeest, antelopes, and zebras. Lionesses tend to kill the medium-sized prey, such as wildebeest and zebra, but would usually be joined by the males to catch the larger prey such as buffalo and giraffe. Lions sometimes also kill elephants. Some of the larger animals they may hunt can be dangerous. Buffalo are very strong and powerful and have been known to kill lions that have been trying to hunt them. If larger prey is scarce, lions might also eat ostrich eggs, birds, and reptiles.

This food web shows how energy flows from one living thing to the next.

Hyena

Lion

Baboon

Zebra

Impala

Grass

Acacia tree

Termite

CAUSE AN UPROAR!

National Geographic's Cause an Uproar campaign aims to stop the population decline in big cats, caused by factors such as habitat loss and **poaching**, by 2015. The campaign encourages people to donate but also provides grants for scientists to help big cats by educating local people about the animals.

Typical meal

A typical meal for lions is 18–20 pounds (8–9 kilograms) of meat, but an adult male can eat up to 75 pounds (34 kilograms) in one go! A lioness can eat more than 55 pounds (25 kilograms). Lions often eat all the food they have caught and then rest for a few days before hunting again. Lions sometimes swallow grass. They then bring it back up again, along with fur balls and any **parasites** that might have been living in their stomachs.

Order of feeding

Despite the fact that the lionesses do most of the hunting, the males get to eat first! They have no reservations about stealing prey from their own pride members. The lionesses eat second and the cubs get whatever is left. This is one reason why many cubs die of starvation, as there is little food left after a hungry pride has eaten their fill.

Lions can go a few days without drinking water. In very dry areas, lions seem to be able to get enough water from the stomach contents of their prey.

Scavenging

Only one kill is made in every five attempts. This often means that lions have to **scavenge** food from other predators' kills. This doesn't just mean stealing food from animals such as hyenas (who can also sometimes chase off lions from a kill if there are enough of them), but also other cats such as cheetahs. If a cheetah has managed to kill a prey animal, it will be exhausted and is therefore no match for even a single lion, who can successfully chase off the smaller cheetah.

Lions might sometimes go for days without eating, so when they do make a kill, they feast!

ANOTHER NAME

Simba means lion in the African language of Swahili. In the Zulu language, *ingonyama* means lion.

What Is a Lion's Life Cycle?

The life cycle of an animal covers its birth to its death and all the different stages in between. A lion's life cycle includes birth, youth, and adulthood. During adulthood they **reproduce** and have young.

Mating

Male lions sniff a female's urine to work out when she may be ready to mate. They may also follow her around for a few days. A male lion's vomeronasal organ is used to detect the scent. There is not usually any fighting over females. Whichever lion reaches the female first tends to stay with her for the four-day period during which she is able to become pregnant. Lions have many partners over their lifetime.

Lions show affection by head rubbing and licking.

This lioness is grooming her young cub.

Pregnancy and birth

Lionesses are pregnant for 3.5 months on average. They can give birth at any time of year but peak time for giving birth is in the rainy season because this is when food is easiest to find. There are usually between one and six cubs born in a litter and they are blind and helpless when first born.

Cubs

Females help each other look after the cubs and cubs can nurse from any female that has recently given birth herself. Cubs are kept hidden by their mother for about 8 weeks, usually in a thicket or a small hill called a kopjes. This is just until they are big enough to join the rest of the pride. During this time, the cubs feed on their mother's milk. They are weaned by the age of 7–10 months.

SPOTTY FUR

Cubs often have light-colored rosette shapes on their fur, particularly on their back legs. These fade as the cub gets older. Lionesses in the Kalahari Desert in southern Africa keep the spots on their lower legs and sometimes on their belly.

Young lions

From about the age of 5–7 months, young lions can be left on their own for over a day while their mother hunts. They don't go out to hunt till they are about a year old. They remain dependent on adults until at least the age of 16 months. Most females stay with the pride they were born into but males usually leave around the age of 2.5 years.

LOW SURVIVAL RATE

Only 1 in 8 cubs make it to adulthood. Starvation as a result of being the last ones to eat after a kill is one factor, but infanticide—being killed by males who have taken over a pride—is another. A quarter of all cub deaths are due to infanticide. If a cub can survive past its second birthday, the chance of living a full life increases dramatically.

The cycle begins again

Lionesses have babies about every two years from an average age of four years old. However, birth can be more frequent if cubs have been killed by rival males. Males can reproduce from the age of about five.

In the wild, females live longer than males. Many males don't live past 10 years old, sometimes due to fights with stronger males, but some have been known to survive to the age of 16. Asiatic males tend to live till 16 more regularly than African lions. Females survive till they are 15–18 years old. Asiatic females can live a bit longer than this.

Adult males do not directly care for their cubs (although they sometimes play with the older ones). However as long as they keep control of the pride, they will avoid their cubs being killed by rival males.

How Do Lions Behave?

Lions are social animals and live in groups of up to 40. These groups are called prides. The average pride has 13 members, the majority of which are related females. Usually, there are only two males in a pride and these will have stolen the pride from older lions. Smaller groups within a pride come and go at different times. It is not often that the whole pride is all together. This is known as a fission-fusion society. There is not usually any fighting within a pride because the ability of lions to seriously injure or kill another lion makes fighting too risky.

Infanticide

Male lions can sometimes group together to form **coalitions** and take over a pride. They not only kill the resident males in the pride but all the cubs too. This is because females nursing cubs will not be ready to mate again till their cubs are at least 18 months old. If the cubs are killed then she can mate within days. The new males want their offspring to be part of the pride rather than that of the old males. Lionesses often try to protect their cubs. This is easier if a number of females have had cubs around the same time—they help each other. Males are a lot bigger than females, so there is often not much hope of saving the cubs.

COALITIONS

If a coalition is made up of two lions, they can usually only control a pride long enough to have one litter of cubs. Bigger coalitions of three or four lions tend to last longer, usually more than three years.

When a coalition of young males tries to take over a pride, the fight can be fatal.

Home range

Lions can live in the same territory or home range for many generations. Male lions mark the boundaries of their home range with urine or sometimes scuff-marks made with their claws. Females will spray urine sometimes, too. Lions roar loudly to put off other lions encroaching on their territory and they will chase any intruders away. The size of a lion's home range varies depending on the amount of prey available. It is usually about 100 square miles (260 square kilometers). In the Kalahari, the lions have home ranges six times larger than lions living elsewhere. One pride was found to range over an area of 1,750 square miles (4,532 square kilometers).

Able to count?

It seems that lions can count. In experiments, scientists played back recorded lion roars to a real group of lions. The real lions only responded by moving towards the recorded lions to challenge them when their group outnumbered the recorded lions by at least two.

Communication

To greet each other, lions rub heads together often with their tails held up in the air. They might also make a moaning sound during their greeting. Lionesses use their tails to signal to their cubs that they should follow her.

Lions climb trees for many reasons, including to find a place to rest.

Roaring is one of the ways that lions communicate.

Tree climbing

Lions climb trees for several reasons, including to avoid the tsetse fly. Some areas have more flies than others, but all over Africa lions climb trees. They may also want a better view of their surroundings or to find a good breeze.

BORN FREE FOUNDATION

The Born Free Foundation works with local people in Kenya to find practical solutions to the problem of lions attacking livestock. This includes education, reinforcing livestock **enclosures**, and knowing which areas to avoid during the day.

A DAY IN THE LIFE OF A LION

A lion's day is made up of hunting, feeding most days, playing, and lots of sleeping!

Sleeping

Lions are mainly nocturnal, meaning they are more active at night and spend most of the day sleeping. This is mainly because the temperature is often very high during the day. Lions become more active in the late afternoon when they tend to socialize with other members of the pride. Lions save energy by doing most of their hunting at night when it is cooler. Their excellent night vision means this is no problem for them.

Working

Female lions do most of the work! Lionesses do most of the hunting, often in teams. However, males can take down bigger prey than the females when they do hunt and they also protect the pride from rival male coalitions.

Lions can rest or sleep for about 20 hours a day!

This lioness is trying to catch a kudu, a type of antelope.

Playing

While adult lions might be having a rest, cubs are happy to play—with each other, their mother's tail, or anything else they can find! They usually copy adult behavior such as stalking. This behavior helps to teach the cubs skills they will need to survive later in life.

GEORGE ADAMSON

George Adamson was a British conservationist known as the "father of lions". He is famous for helping to return Christian the lion back to the wild. Christian was legally bought from Harrods department store in London in 1969. When he got too big for his owners, he was moved to an enclosure at another couple's home. Later he was flown to Kenya and returned to the wild by Adamson. George's wife, Joy Adamson, wrote Born Free to tell the story.

How Intelligent Are Lions?

One of the main ways in which lions show their intelligence is in the skills they use for hunting. Many prey animals can run faster than lions and can sustain that speed too. So lions have developed two main ways of hunting. The first involves stalking the prey animal by creeping closer from one area of cover to another, staying hidden till no more than 150 feet (about 45 meters) away, and then bursting out to ambush the animal.

The second method involves going to an area where they know prey will pass by and just waiting. Lions are patient enough to do this successfully.

CRAIG PACKER

Craig Packer is a conservationist and author. He began his career researching baboons and monkeys, but in 1978, he went to Tanzania to become head of the Serengeti Lion Project. As part of his research, one of his experiments involved showing pretend life-sized lions with different colors and lengths of mane to real lions and monitoring their response. Female lions all went for the ones with darker manes, while males seemed less intimidated to attack the lighter ones. When Packer looked at real life lions, those with darker manes were more likely to heal well from injuries and sire more healthy cubs. Those with lighter colored manes were more likely to get sick. Darker maned lions are the most desirable mates and fearsome enemies.

Teamwork for lions is essential when hunting animals bigger and faster than themselves.

Teamwork

Females often hunt together—teamwork is important when trying to catch bigger or more difficult prey. One strategy used involves one or two lions forcing a herd of animals to run into the path of experienced lion hunters. Lions are also more successful when there is no moon because they have much better vision than most of their prey.

35

What Threats Do Lions Face?

Lions face many threats, most of which are a result of human behavior.

Habitat loss

One of the main problems for lions is loss of habitat. A constant growth in the human population means land that lions once roamed is now being transformed into homes, farms, and ranches for people.

Even today, lions are still used in circus performances. In order for the lions to be persuaded to perform tricks, their trainers often use many forms of mistreatment such as beating or withholding food or water.

CIRCUS LIONS

In December 2010, 25 ex-circus lions were rescued from Bolivia. A UK conservation group, Animal Defenders International, told of the horrendous living conditions of circus animals in South America. As a result, the Bolivian government passed a law saying that no more animals were allowed in circuses. The rescued lions were eventually given a home in Colorado.

Killed by people

Lions are killed by farmers after their livestock has been attacked. This happens more often nowadays because humans are taking over land that was part of lion ranges. Where villagers might once have shot only the individual "nuisance" lion, they are now poisoning whole prides.

Lions are also among the large numbers of wild animals that are being caught in snares and sold as bushmeat for people to eat. This was once a way for individuals to provide food for their family, but it is now an international trade. Nearly 7,500 tons of bushmeat arrives illegally in the UK every year. Some of this meat is disguised as beef.

Inbreeding

Another problem for lions is inbreeding, where many generations of lions are bred from the same small group. This can happen as prides become more and more isolated. Inbreeding can cause birth deformities and a gradual weakening of the species. However, it is possible to reintroduce lions from another area to widen the possibilities for breeding.

Disease

Diseases such as tuberculosis have killed hundreds of lions in South Africa. The disease is thought to be spread by lions eating infected buffalo. Feline Immunodeficiency Virus, closely related to Human Immunodeficiency Virus (HIV), is a problem for lions whose immune systems have been weakened by other diseases. Some forms of disease can be caused indirectly by humans. The canine distemper disaster of 1994 was thought to have been spread by domestic dogs that live in nearby villages. The disease caused the deaths of more than a third of the lions living in the Serengeti in Africa.

Hunting

Lions are one of the "big five" wild animals that tourists like to see when on safari. The term "big five" comes from the time they were one of the five most popular animals to shoot. Nowadays, "trophy hunting" continues. Lion skin rugs, necklaces from lion's teeth, and other such trophies are desired by some people. In fact, two-thirds (64 percent of 5,663 lions) of lions hunted for sport were shipped to the United States between 1999 and 2008.

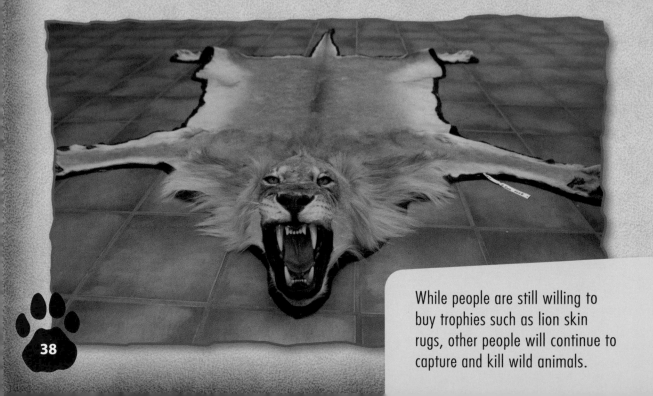

While people are still willing to buy trophies such as lion skin rugs, other people will continue to capture and kill wild animals.

Many people believe that keeping wild animals such as lions in cages is cruel.

Canned hunting is a legal practice where lions are bred specifically for hunting. There are about 3,000 lions held captive for this purpose in South Africa. They are often sedated and kept in enclosed areas (with electric fencing) so that they cannot escape from the hunters. In 2010, the Supreme Court in South Africa ruled that canned hunting can continue legally.

LOSS OF RANGE

Lions have disappeared from over 80 percent of their historic range. They are now extinct in 26 countries.

How Can People Help Lions?

Fitting a radio collar to a lion allows researchers to discover more about lions' daily lives.

Lions are in danger of dying out and a big part of the problem is humans. However, people can also help to protect lions and their habitats.

Conservation organizations

Improving public knowledge and understanding about lions is an important part of what conservation groups do. Conservationists encourage local people to want to protect their local wildlife and their habitats. Research into how lions live will make it easier for conservationists to come up with plans to help lions survive.

Eco-tourism

Eco-tourism can be used to help lions by providing an alternative source of income for local people. Many tourists are interested in seeing animals in the wild but often need a guide to show them where to go and how to behave with the animals. Local people can do this job and other jobs linked to tourism.

What can you do?

If you want to help save lions, there are many things you can do. You could donate some pocket money, join a conservation group, such as WWF, or even sponsor a lion. Telling family and friends what you have read about in this book and on the internet will help—the more people who care about the fate of lions, the more likely a change can be made.

This researcher is measuring a lioness's teeth.

NEW SUBSPECIES?

Scientists have used DNA to prove that lions in Addis Ababa Zoo in Ethiopia are genetically different from any other populations for which **genetic** information is available. These lions have very large, dark manes unlike any other lions known. The researchers have called for urgent conservation efforts to make sure these lions don't become extinct.

What Does the Future Hold for Lions?

Sadly, lions and other big cats are facing more and more threats to their survival. The IUCN red list shows the survival status of many animals. Some lion subspecies are already extinct in the wild. Lions are generally listed as vulnerable but in West and Central Africa they are **endangered**. Lions are hit hardest in West Africa because governments have no **incentives** to protect them—eco-tourism is only just starting to become common in West Africa, so lions don't have much economic value at the moment.

The people problem

The future is not good for lions as they lose habitat due to human population growth. The fall in the lion population has been dramatic in recent years and it is still falling. In contrast, the human population is increasing, so yet more land will be needed for crops and livestock.

On the positive side, there are many conservation groups around the world working to protect lions and their habitats. Television programs and campaigns highlighting the plight of lions will hopefully encourage more people to help.

It is important that we don't allow lions to die out. They deserve their place in the natural world. The more young people—like you—who get involved, the better. Every little bit helps.

AMY DICKMAN

Amy Dickman is a British researcher who has worked to protect carnivores in Africa for over 14 years. She is the director of the Ruaha Carnivore Project in Tanzania, where she has been working to try to reduce conflict between local communities and big cats, as well as finding out more about the carnivore population in the area.

Lions are facing a struggle to survive in the wild.

Lion Profile

Species:	Lion
Latin name:	*Panthera leo*
Weight:	Males weigh 326–470 pounds (148–213 kilograms); Females weigh 220–360 pounds (100–164 kilograms)
Length:	Males reach 5.9–6.9 feet (1.8–2.1 meters) in length; Females can grow to 4.9 feet (1.5 meters) in length
Number of young:	Lions usually give birth to one to six cubs every two years. Pregnancy lasts about 3.5 months.
Life expectancy in the wild (average):	15–18 years for females; 10–16 years for males. The oldest known lion was 30!
Habitat:	Mainly sub-Saharan Africa and the Gir Forest, India

Sensitive eyes help the lion see well in the dark.

Lions have excellent hearing.

Light brown fur provides good camouflage in dry grass.

Whiskers help the lion find its way when hunting at night.

A male lion's mane offers protection in fights, and also shows his position in the pride.

Strong front legs and powerful shoulder muscles help the lion catch and hold onto large prey.

Glossary

adapt change to suit conditions and surroundings

albino living thing that has no color in its skin or hair

captivity being kept in a zoo or reserve

coalition group of two to six male lions

conservationist someone who helps to protect animals, plants, and habitats

domestic tame and kept by people

eco-tourism form of tourism where people go to see wildlife and help to protect nature

enclosure area of land surrounded by fencing

endangered when a plant or animal is in danger of dying out

evolve change over time

extinct no longer existing

genetics study of characteristics passed from parent to offspring

groom clean the fur and skin

incentive something that causes people to act in a certain way

livestock farm animals

nocturnal active at night

parasite animal that lives on or in another animal and feeds off it without giving anything in return

poaching illegally hunting animals on land that does not belong to the person poaching

predator animal that hunts and eats other animals

prey animal that is hunted and eaten by another animal

reproduce to have offspring

reserve area of protected land set aside for wild animals

retractable capable of being drawn back in to the body

scavenge feed on dead animals that have been killed by another predator

social living in communities or groups, in which relationships are maintained

species group of organisms that are similar and are able to produce offspring together

stalk to hunt by creeping along quietly and secretly

territory area of land that an animal views as its own

Find Out More

Books

Joubert, Beverly and Dereck. *Face to Face with Lions*. Des Moines, Iowa: National Geographic, 2008.

Meinking, Mary. *Lion vs. Gazelle* (Predator Vs. Prey). Chicago: Raintree, 2011.

Shiekh-Miller, Jonathan. *Big Cats*. London, UK: Usborne, 2008.

Websites

www.bbc.co.uk/nature/life/lion
This BBC website has lots of videos featuring lions.

www.kids.nationalgeographic.co.uk/kids/animals/creaturefeature/lion
Learn more about lions and see a video of a male roaring.

Organizations

Panthera
www.panthera.org
Panthera is a conservation organization that works to protect big cats such as lions.

WWF
www.wwf.org
WWF works to protect animals and nature and needs your help! Have a look at their website and see what you can do.

Index